Poetry:
Telling It Like It Is

Poetry:
Telling It Like It Is

B. J. Moore

VANTAGE PRESS
New York

FIRST EDITION

Published by Vantage Press, Inc.
516 West 34th Street, New York, New York 10001

Manufactured in the United States of America
ISBN: 0-533-11375-X

Library of Congress Catalog Card No.: 94-90807

0 9 8 7 6 5 4 3 2 1

To
W. Basirah TaHa

You are my awesome wonder, Wanda,
You are my seven rolls of the dice;
If I should live my life all over
You will be my number one twice.

The poems "Black Pride," "Mother, the All in All," and "Happy (Eighty-fifth) Birthday" are inspired by, written for, and dedicated to my mother,
Mrs. Ethel Collins Green.

"Imani" is dedicated to my little great-grand goddaughter, Imani Salaam, December 27, 1992.

"The Gift" is dedicated to Matthew Joseph Cousin, the second son of my pastor, Rev. David B. Cousin Sr., and his lovely wife, Mrs. Valerie E. Cousin, January 18, 1993.

"A Done Deal" is dedicated to Douglas Jerome Goodson, born July 14, 1946; he won a Purple Heart during the Vietnam conflict; he expired September 18, 1993.

Contents

Poetry:
Telling It Like It Is

My Prayer

There was a time when we knelt to pray.
We did not know what to say.
We just thanked the Lord for his goodness,
And thanked him for another day.

It was not for form or fashion,
Nor to see who had the longest say,
But to thank him for our daily bread,
And to forgive our sin each day.

Thank you, Lord, for the sunshine,
An extra thanks for the rain.
Thank you for cooling the fever.
And thank you for easing the pain.

Thank you for all your lovely gifts,
That you have bestowed upon us.
Thank you for wisdom and understanding.
Please forgive us for our lust.

Thank you for all of our loved ones.
Teach us that unconditioned love
For all our friends and neighbors,
Most of all, you, O Lord, above.

Teach us to forgive, O Lord,
But, dear Lord, above all else,
To love you above our very being,
And our neighbors as ourselves.

Lord, you know our every want,
But please supply our needs.
Please take away the lust and hate,
The biases, prejudices, and greeds.

Replace them with patience and understanding
And a heart like our Father above.
Faith, hope, and charity,
And each day a little more love.

Give us that old-time religion
That shows in our daily walk,
That can be felt when we sing and pray,
And heard when we talk.

Give us that special kind of love
That runs from heart to heart,
The spirit that walks and talks with us,
Until in death we do part.

Forgive us, Lord, day by day,
For all our evil thoughts and sin.
Teach us to love and forgive
Our sisters and brothers time and again.

Then, Lord, when it comes to me,
Please humble me most of all.
Thank you, forgive me, teach me.
Please catch me if I should fall.

Amen.

The Greatest Faith

Jesus hung upon the cross
Between two guilty men.
They were known for being thieves,
And maybe even greater sin.

One of the felons beside the Savior,
Was very loud and profane.
Had heard of no wrong, Jesus had done.
He didn't even know him by name.

He said, "If you are the savior as they say,
Do one thing, if nothing else.
Come down from this cross, and save us,
Then save yourself."

Then there was the other felon,
Hanging on the other side,
Thinking of the wrongs he had done,
Forgetting all about self and pride.

Not questioning, for one moment,
All the things they said Jesus done.
Just knowing deep down in his heart,
He is the Savior, he is God's son.

He wasn't sure this was the same man,
From listening to what the people said.
Blessed two fish and five little loaves,
And thousands of people were fed.

In other times he never cared,
If the sayings were wrong or right.
If this was the man who healed the sick,
And restored the blind man's sight.

This thief was not a fisherman,
So to him it did not matter
Whether or not Jesus calmed a sea,
Or walked upon the water.

He had not heard of the incident
Of Jesus speaking out loud,
Of a bleeding woman touching him,
In the midst of a maddening crowd.

He did remember something about a story
That he really didn't understand,
About Lazarus being raised from the dead,
But is this the man?

The thief could understand his punishment,
For the things that he had done.
But why punish Jesus so severely,
For he had done no wrong?

He never thought of testing Jesus,
To see if the sayings were true.
His only thought as he hung there was,
Jesus, what can I do?

As he hung there on the cross,
With dying faith that the world could see,
He cried, "Jesus, when you reach your kingdom,
Oh, please remember me."

Master's Plan

Live your best in this world,
That's part of the Master's plan.
Live yesterday, die today,
Tomorrow you will rise again.

Give and share and be your best,
Enjoy all things at your hand.
For you lived yesterday, died today,
But tomorrow you will rise again.

Steer a child down the right path,
Pick the abused up out of the mire.
Help a destitute realize a dream,
Fulfill someone's heart's desire.

Take the first step up the unclimbable mountain.
Take on a project you don't understand.
Work yesterday, rest today,
Tomorrow you'll be revived again.

Speak inspiringly to the down and out,
Lift up a spirit with a smile.
Be misused then, abused now,
You'll be rewarded after a while.

Keep reaching for the unreachable star.
Don't for a second think you can't.
Don't try yesterday, today you won't
And tomorrow you shan't.

Just like the Bible says,
You will reap just what you sow.
Plant it yesterday, tend it today.
And tomorrow it will grow.

Daily we walk through the shadows of death.
That too is the Master's plan.
Each time we died, but still we tried,
Knowing that we will rise again.

We are the greatest of God's creations.
We are His master plan.
Yesterday we stepped out, today we fell,
But tomorrow we will rise again.

Church

I visited a church a few weeks ago
To fellowship and pray a prayer.
It was a good thing I took Jesus with me,
Or he never would have gotten there.

At first I thought I was at a fashion show,
Trying to keep my eyes straight ahead;
While the latest creations passed me by,
Big hats, but bigger heads.

When the deacon went to the altar to pray,
In relief I bowed my head.
His God had to have a Ph.D.
To understand what he said.

That choir was really on fire,
Praising God from the top of their lungs.
They screamed out the hymns so loud,
You couldn't understand a word of the songs.

One thing there was no doubt about,
Never a delay, or reason to hesitate.
About every quarter of an hour.
They were passing the collection plate.

Then came God's chosen one.
He got up to preach the word.
Chose his text, began to speak.
I could not believe what I heard.

He spoke about a neighboring church
In another nearby town not very far;
About how well that pastor dressed
And about his brand new car.

Finally he opened the doors of the church.
One thing he made very clear.
If you were not of the upper crust,
You definitely do not belong here.

When it was over I said, "Thank you, Jesus."
When I got outside I prayed a prayer.
I said, "Thank you, Jesus, for coming with me.
Otherwise you would not have been here."

Women, Enough Is Enough

Women, don't you realize
That enough, is enough, is enough?
Since forever we've been men's footstool;
We've taken enough of their huff.

We had to stay home and have the babies,
Mend their clothes and scrub the floors.
Be mama when they want to cry,
And do all of their unwanted chores.

We have to walk two steps behind them,
Keep their egos boosted high,
Keep our noses to the grindstone,
And we're not allowed to ask why.

You've got to be a sex machine,
Under any and all conditions.
When and where, and why and how,
Is usually his decision.

If for some reason he falls short,
And you have to seek employment,
To fill up the spaces he can't fill,
He calls that your enjoyment.

So you leave home each and every day,
Trying to help him make ends meet,
Eight hours fighting with a boss,
On a job that's not too sweet.

Eight hours on a boring job,
Hours working at home on your feet.
Endless hours with kids and homework,
Then hours with him on the sheet.

You take a back seat on the job,
Then from husband and kids, it's tough.
Then compare your paycheck to the men's.
Then you know enough, is enough, is enough.

If you choose to comfortably wear jeans,
That are cut off above the knee,
If this upsets the men you pass.
That's your own fault, you see.

If he becomes so excited he rapes you,
Legally that's a shame.
But don't be surprised when you go to court,
And they tell you, that you are to blame.

So if you think that is hard,
And that living in a man's world is tough,
It won't get better until you realize
That enough, is enough, is enough.

Normally, we're just bitches and whores,
Abusing those nice men we vamp,
But try to rise above them.
Then we're sluts, we're dirt and tramps.

So if we're ever to be recognized,
Or be equal in this man's nation,
We've got to go to the Ivy League schools,
And get a manly education.

Get on up, go to the polls and vote,
Do whatever it takes to make a dent.
There is no logical reason on earth,
Why a woman can't be president.

So in order to accomplish something,
Stop taking just any kind of stuff.
Take a stand, and let men know,
That enough, is enough, is enough.

Tonight's the Night

You say I've got to go home with you;
You have music I have never heard.
This music is so out of sight,
It can't be described with words.

You say this music is so unique,
It will knock me off my feet.
Tell me just where will I land,
On your sofa, or on your sheet?

So you've planned an early breakfast;
It'll be so romantic, just me and you.
That sounds like you will be the diner,
And I will be the menu.

You say this will be such a great date,
That I won't believe my eyes.
I'll be like a kid on Christmas morning,
Surprise after surprise after surprise.

You say if I should blow this date,
That's something I will live to regret.
Thanks, you said the magic word *live*.
Live, that's something I won't forget.

You say you have rum from the islands,
And delicacies ordered in.
You sound like you planned this night,
For you, and a special friend.

Your offer sounds so tempting.
I hate to spoil the plans you've made.
Taking a new stranger home every night,
Are you sure you don't have AIDS?

Sugar

You used to call me sweet names,
And I thought that it was grand.
That made me want to be oh, so nice,
Because you were such a wonderful man.

You always opened doors for me,
And gentlemanly tipped your hat.
You never forgot to hold my chair,
Until I was comfortably sat.

I was the happiest woman on earth;
I was the envy of everyone's eye.
I never saw the smirk on their face,
When we went strolling by.

Your excuses were unquestionable,
Whenever you broke a date.
I thought it was blind love for me,
Whenever you showed up real late.

I was always awed by the things you did,
You've done everything so well.
You could have told me anything;
You had me completely under your spell.

But just as fate would have it,
The right play, but the wrong scene.
There I saw you, my love, my king,
Being royal to your other queen.

So I decided to do it your way,
Mingle, let another man tell me a lie.
But you say sweet women don't do that,
But still you can't tell me why.

Yes, I still love you very much,
But why should I be by myself?
When you go out with your other queen,
Then I go out with someone else.

But now I too know the secret,
The manners, the action and dialect.
You get practice with the others,
So with me you are perfect.

Now that I know your secret,
Of all those lovely things you do.
I never thought you would be so upset,
At me getting some practice too.

You no longer call me sweet things.
I am no longer your sugar and spice.
And being the gentleman you are,
That new name is not so nice.

You are still my gentleman,
Now it seems I'm an unscratchable itch.
I can see the frown when you call me sweet,
When you want to call me bitch.

My Devilish/Angelic Woman

I have this devilish/angelic woman.
I think she is straight out of hell.
She has me wrapped around her little finger.
Solely and bodily by hook, crook or spell.

Because I have this woman,
And she's living right here.
She is the living devil.
But she's so sweet and dear.

My friends say she has rooted me,
And I believe they are right.
Because I am as evil as a junkyard dog,
When I'm alone at night.

She's sterner than my mother,
She works me harder than my boss.
But when she makes love to me,
My body and soul are lost.

If you want to see an evil man,
Or run into your worst foe,
See me tomorrow morning
If last night, that woman said no.

When she wants, she treats me like a boy,
but she loves me like a man.
There are so many things about that woman
That I just don't understand.

She took the house and the children.
Now she wants all the loot.
She's not the prettiest woman on earth,
So she must have a root.

Women are so much fun to love.
They can be your very best friends.
But when she wants, she'll throw you out,
And reel you back in again.

The way to a man's heart is through his stomach,
but ham and eggs are not a must.
But that web she spins around that bed,
You have got to have or bust.

You can call it root if you want to.
You can call it hex or spell.
Whatever it is that woman has,
She really uses it well.

Appointment

Up bright and early this morning.
Have an appointment I have to keep.
Can't take time for breakfast,
And definitely didn't have enough sleep.

Rub-a-dub-dub, a skip through the tub.
Thank God I had laid out my clothes.
Now find matching shoes and bag.
What's this, a run in my panty hose?

Take your time, slow down, relax,
You're doing okay so far.
Pocketbook, briefcase in hand,
Now where are the keys to the car?

Okay, now take it easy,
Just let your mind go blank.
What did you do when you came in?
You have to stop and think.

I kicked off my shoes when I came in,
Then grabbed a candy mint,
And fell asleep sitting there,
Thinking about this appointment.

I woke up feeling a bit relaxed,
And happy the day was over.
Aha, that must be where the keys are,
Between the pillows of the sofa.

Well, at last I'm out of the house;
Talking about relieved, I am.
Oh no, I can't believe my eyes;
Oh, please, not a traffic jam.

So at love's long last, I finally arrive.
Thank God for self-control.
Things like murder come to mind,
When you hear what I was told.

"I am sorry to have to tell you this;
Mr. Johnson was called away.
I will have to reschedule your appointment,
For some other day."

Diet or Dead

I went to the doctor the other day.
I told him, "Something has to be done.
Carrying all this fat around,
Believe me, it's no fun."

He said, "Take it easy, take your time.
Don't let this drive you out of your head.
Eat a lot less, exercise more.
Being fat is different from dead."

It seems all the world's on a diet today.
Everybody's going out of their head.
True fat is unattractive.
But fat is not dead.

You can fight obesity.
Refuse that extra piece of pie or bread.
You can back away from the table.
But you can't come back from the dead.

Obesity leads to blood pressure problems,
Sugar diabetes and other things.
Fat is not picky or choosy.
It can happen to a pauper or a king.

Exercise is a curse word.
It's a pain far below the neck.
But getting fat is so much fun.
You'll worry about it later by heck.

But later comes sooner than you think.
You can tell by those clothes you wore.
You can no longer buy at the petite shop.
Now you go to the fat folks' store.

Now you're stealing candy, grapes, and peanuts
While you're shopping in the grocery store.
Your grocery bill used to be moderate,
And inflation is not the only reason it's more.

You used to jog around the block
But now you're out of whack.
Now any discomfort you feel from exertion,
"Oh, God, don't let this be a heart attack."

Your mirror even lies on you.
And getting dressed just makes you mad.
As much money as you pay for your clothes now,
How in the world can you look this bad?

Now it's time for that end-all, be-all diet;
Take a pill, exercise, and it's gone.
But don't be shocked when you wake up,
And that fat is still hanging on.

So now it's time for the overnight diet.
Don't eat; don't drink. Just lose the fat.
But beware, you didn't put it on that fast
And losing it won't be as easy as that.

Just push back from that table
And remember what the doctor said.
Take your time and take it off.
There is a difference in fat and dead.

Doctor's Office

Sitting in the doctor's office.
My God, what a bore, and pain.
If it wasn't for my aches and fever,
I would not come here again.

Looking around at the patients,
Listening to them grunt and groan.
I wonder if they're as ill as I,
Or just like to complain and moan.

I know there are hypochondriacs,
All kind of fakers everywhere.
I know if they took a good laxative
They wouldn't even have to be here.

I wonder if those heart patients knew—
And this remedy is tried and true:
Just take a good dose of baking soda,
Get rid of the gas, and feel like new.

Some swear they never heard of Ben-Gay;
They are lying and that's a sin.
Will come to the doctor with a hangnail,
The day I have to come in.

At last I get in to see the doctor,
And the shock, to my dismay.
"I am so glad you came in now.
You wouldn't have lasted another day."

"Doc, I woke up with a minor headache,
Came in to get some pills.
Now you're trying to tell me,
That I am deathly ill."

I am in for consultation,
To put my mind at ease.
This charlatan is trying to tell me,
I have a deadly disease.

Thank God for second opinions,
But doctors now I truly dread.
One says call the undertaker,
The other says I will live instead.

Now I am really all shook up,
And not really sure of what to do.
One doctor says you're at death's door,
The other says you're as good as new.

So I went to see one more doctor;
I was filled with hope and doubt.
He said to me, "You're in good health,
And there's nothing to worry about."

So I left the doctor's office;
I was feeling really swell.
I'll take a laxative and baking soda,
And tell the doctors to go to hell.

—*The following three poems are dedicated to*

Mrs. Ethel Green.

God Bless.

Mom, I will always love you.

Black Pride

Is it really necessary,
That I stand out in a crowd?
And yell as loud as I can,
That I am black and proud?

Being proud I will show it,
By being the best that I can be.
Being black you will know it.
You have but to look and see.

Pride is plain ego,
So color me woman,
In a world of hate and bigotry,
Trying to be the best I can.

If I had the last match in the world,
And all the light went out,
Should I stand and yell, "I have a match,"
Or strike it and let the world find out.

If I do some good, and make my mark,
Whatever in life that be,
I would want the world to wonder who,
Not what color is she.

Mother, the All in All

From the day of conception,
Mother is food, clothes, shelter, and air.
She is water, heat, love, and comfort.
She is your world, your song and prayer.

At birth she is a deliverer,
A blanket, protection from the cold.
She also is a teacher
When the mysteries of life unfold.

She teaches you to eat and drink,
To walk and talk and care;
To beware of the harmful things,
To live to play and share.

Mother is the world's greatest doctor.
She cools the fever and eases the aches.
She kisses away all the pain,
And puts Band-Aids on the scrapes.

Mother is the fairest playmate;
She shares the toys with you.
She teaches you the A,B,Cs,
And how to play peek-a-boo.

Mother is oftentimes the father.
She teaches you how to play ball;
How to run, to jump and catch,
How to knock that ball over the wall,

She protects you from the bullies,
The bugs, worms, and the like.
She finds time during her busy day,
To teach you to ride a bike.

Mother goes out to earn a living,
To keep her family together.
Facing all kind of bias situations,
In all kinds of weather.

As you grow older you realize,
Mother is your best friend.
She will stand by you, no matter what,
Through the thick and thin.

She teaches you about God and faith,
About trust, love, and prayer.
She wants you to know there is comfort,
Even when she can't be there.

She sends you to the best of schools
To prepare you to be your best,
Knowing the world is full of challenges
To prepare you for each test.

Mother tells you about relationships,
About true love and pain.
How love can bring so much happiness,
But it can also cause you pain.

Mother is a lawyer.
Whether you are right or wrong,
She is there as your defender,
No matter what the crime, or how long.

As time takes its toll on Mother,
She sits back and listens, she's wise.
She knows when to quietly listen,
And when to advise.

Happy (Eighty-fifth) Birthday

Happy eighty-fifth birthday, Mrs. Ethel Green.
I wish you so many more.
Many more hearty and healthy years,
And great-grandchildren by the score.

It has always been such a pleasure
To greet your smiling face.
To listen to your words of wisdom,
And absorb your amazing grace.

I watched you age graciously
And courageously over the years.
Through ups and downs, ins and outs,
Through your laughter and your tears.

You have a beautiful sense of humor.
Truly, Mrs. Green, you are great.
She tells me I'm not eighty-five;
I am the flip side of fifty-eight.

Happy birthday, happy birthday,
I am truly elated, you see,
While making out your distinguished list
You happened to remember me.

Thank God for you, and God bless you,
And be with you your whole life through.
I pray when I turn eighty-five,
To be as grand and gracious as you.

   Happy eighty-fifth birthday

That's What Grandmothers Are For

To all grand- and great-grandmothers

When everything is going wrong,
And there is no relief in sight.
I can always go to my grandmother;
Together we put up a good fight.

She always finds time to listen
No matter what the problem is.
There is a handkerchief in her apron,
Whenever there are tears.

She keeps a Band-Aid handy,
Whenever I scrape my knee.
Her kisses are better than medicine;
Anyway they work for me.

She never needs any money.
My reward is in the cookie jar.
I know that cooking is high on the list
Of things that grandmothers are for.

When I spend the night with Grandmother,
And we kneel down to pray.
I listen to her when she thanks the Lord,
And ask, "Grandmother, what should I say?"

She told me, "You just say, 'Thank you, Lord,
And forgive me for me sin.'
Always keep your heart open,
So when He knocks, you just let Him in."

When everything is gloomy,
My grandmother is my shining star.
Then I remember her words in prayer,
And what grandmothers are for.

When I see a bouquet of flowers,
Or ripe vegetables on a vine,
Or smell fried chicken and corn bread,
My grandmother always come to mind.

One thing my grandmother told me:
"Try to be the best at whatever you do.
People easily forget the good you've done
But the bad, always comes back to you."

I will never forget my grandmother,
And praise the God behind her star.
And each day I add something to the list
Of things that grandmothers are for.

You're Getting Old

When walking through a five and dime
Becomes a scary walk through a maze.
Because you don't know what is a toy
Or what's for real these days.

Stop into a sporting store;
Ask to see some tennis shoes.
They're not tennises; they're sneakers.
You're outdated; you've got the blues.

When eavesdropping on a teen conversation,
Your ears start to fold,
Everything they speak today is Greek,
Then you know you're getting old.

When you go walking in the park
And all the walkers pass you by.
You're walking as fast as you can.
Still you're left behind; you wonder why.

You treat yourself to a movie.
God forbid you take a friend.
Buy your popcorn and find a seat;
Fall asleep before the main feature begins.

Everyone's casually dressed for a picnic.
And you're wrapped up because you're cold.
Your radiator is cooling down;
Then you know you are getting old.

When fried chicken and potato salad
Find a noticeable place to turn to fat.
Old age is moving in.
And you can be sure of that.

When you change your fragrant roll-on
To a minty, smelly, rub-on balm
And arthritis is your faithful companion,
Now it's time for alarm.

When your only goal becomes heaven,
And you stop chasing that pot of gold
When your throne become a rocking chair,
Then you're there, not getting old.

Never Satisfied

While in my mother's womb listening,
I learned how to pray.
In my very first prayer I said,
"Lord, let me see a birthday."

Finally that day arrived.
Thank God, at last I am here.
I can feel, smell, taste, and see,
And even shed a tear.

Now, Lord, I ask for one more thing;
Please make me big and strong.
Help me stand, walk, and talk,
And teach me right from wrong.

Now that I am walking and talking,
Look at the things I'm getting into.
I'm trying to be patient as I can,
But when I'm ten, here's what will I do.

I know when I am ten years old,
I can do many things myself.
I can ride a bike, go to the store,
And do things for someone else.

Ten years old is kinda nice,
But there is so much to be seen.
There are some things I can't do now,
But wait till I am a teen.

Thank you, Lord, for being with me,
Because being a teen is fun.
But I'm really going to live it up.
When I am twenty-one.

Oh my, the roaring twenties;
It's so good to be alive.
But it is said, you reach your peak,
When you turn thirty-five.

Thirty-five is really great,
I guess it's where I should be.
But everyone that is anyone
knows that life begins at forty.

Forty is the age to be,
And everything is grand.
I worked hard and saved myself;
I've got the world in my hand.

Oh, Lord, here comes fifty.
So what, there is nothing wrong.
I am still as happy as I can be.
I'm hale, hearty, and strong.

Hey, wait a minute; I am sixty.
Lord, do me favor, if you can.
Turn back the hands of time
And make me thirty once again.

Seventy is knocking on my door.
I have pains, doubts, and fears.
Lord, I would be so grateful
If I could call back some years.

Lord, I want to thank you,
For being by my side.
No matter what age I was,
I was never satisfied.

Now that I am eighty,
With only time and wisdom to give,
Lord, I ask you one more thing:
Please just let me live.

Imani

Thank you, dear God, for giving me
This most beautiful gift in the world,
This precious warm, sweet, and loving,
Beautiful baby girl.

As I look into her beautiful eyes,
A fright comes into my heart.
You entrusted her into my care.
Now I must do my part.

Please walk and talk and stay with me
As I love and teach her day by day.
To be as great as she can be,
For this I daily pray.

Please help me always to make the time
To hear her happiness and her pain.
Teach me how to teach her the beauty
Of the sunshine and the rain.

Help me to live the kind of life
That if she chooses to emulate me
Whatever she does will be good and right
That she will be proud for the world to see.

Help me to be her closest friend
So that she can always count on me;
And trust my wisdom and judgment
Whatever her problem may be.

I love you, my little baby girl,
You will always be number one to me.
Nothing or no one can take your place.
You are my Imani.

The Gift

Thank you, dear God, for giving me,
This beautiful bundle of joy.
It's as heavenly as an angel,
As delicate as a toy.

With perfect little fingers and toes,
A cute little mouth and nose,
Beautiful clear and eager eyes,
To guide him wherever he goes.

Thank you, God, for trusting me,
Though I cannot do it alone.
Stay by my side, help me to teach
Him until he is fully grown.

I will teach him to read the Bible,
But first of all how to pray.
How to live by, and understand your word,
And trust he does not stray.

Honor all fathers, mothers, and elders,
Love friends and neighbors as himself.
But to honor the greatest commandment of all:
Love you above all else.

Never to lie, cheat or steal,
O God, lest he fall.
Rather than speak cruelly to a friend,
Never to utter a word at all.

Teach him to be brave like David,
To put all of his trust in you.
Strive to be the very best,
At everything he puts his mind to.

Dear Lord, don't let him falter,
Trying to emulate the man in me.
Make him humble and righteous like you.
That will be my thanks to thee.

Follow That Tot

As far back as I can remember,
Back when I was a tot,
I reckoned, plotted, planned, and schemed,
Imagined and dreamed a lot.

As soon as I get out these of pampers,
And get to head-start school,
I know I will be the best one there;
I will be first to learn the golden rule.

Now that I'm in head start,
It's not all I hoped it would be.
They won't let me build a skyscraper,
So on to kindergarten for me.

So on to kindergarten I went,
At least that was a start.
A B Cs and one to ten,
But that's not very smart.

Here I am in grade school,
The smartest kid you've ever seen.
I'm getting bigger every day;
Very soon I'll be a teen.

A teenager and I'm in junior high,
And I have learned a lot.
You won't believe a few years back,
I was a dreaming scheming tot.

Library, sports, dating, and dancing,
I've waited for that so long.
Proms, parties, and the opposite sex,
I am really moving on.

College, growing up, facing the world,
My first time leaving home.
Making decisions, balancing budgets;
I am really on my own.

Higher education, did I finally arrive?
Is this as far as I go?
Not if you're going to follow your dream.
Each day you learn more and more.

There is no end to learning;
Just live, you will learn a lot.
Or you will no longer be
That dreaming, scheming tot.

My Child

I carried you in my womb.
I loved and nourished you there.
I shared my all and all with you,
My God, my song, my prayer.

I kept you warm and fed you;
I walked and talked with you.
I told you of my thought and plans,
And the things I wanted for you.

Then the blessed day arrived;
They placed you in my arms.
I loved you from head to toe,
And all your baby charms.

I placed you in your cradle.
I rocked you by night and day.
I cooed, sang, and played with you,
And chased your fears away.

I cried your first day of school,
Because too soon you would be gone.
I pray your dreams will be fulfilled.
Before time for you to move on.

I stood back and admired you,
In your first formal wear.
This was the beginning of your journey,
On your trip to everywhere.

Then I waved you off to college,
Your trip through the looking glass.
To train your mind, sharpen your skills,
And put you in a higher class.

I glowed with love and pride for you
When you walked in your cap and gown.
It's time for me to stand back and watch.
At last you're on solid ground.

We celebrated your very first job
When you started your career.
Thank God now as a mother,
I can shed a joyful tear.

Though we had our ups and downs,
We were happy, I must say.
Oh no, I can't believe this.
You're preparing for your wedding day.

Life has been very good to me.
Fate dealt me a very good hand.
I feel I am living on a cloud,
Because soon I will be a grand.

Watching your grand toddle around
Is like a brand new birth.
Watching it grow, loving it so,
is one of the greatest things on earth.

I wish all the best in the world for you,
As you travel down the road I have trod.
Open each door when opportunity knocks,
And put your trust in God.

I have lived my life to the fullest.
I took; I shared; I gave.
Now it's your turn to live, my child.
Soon I will be going to my grave.

Advertise

A kid took a car the other day,
With no criminal intent.
He accidentally released the brake,
And down the road it went.

From watching his parents drive the car,
Automatically grabbed the wheel.
He hit the gas pedal on the floor,
With the back of his heel.

He was scared to death, in the driver's seat,
And really didn't know what to do,
Praying to God not to panic;
And please help him see it through.

Thank God the traffic wasn't heavy,
And the steering was not hard.
But how did he get into that fix?
He found that very odd.

As he began to get control,
He started to sense the thrill.
But he knew as soon as he got home,
Surely he would get killed.

With one foot on the gas.
And the other on the brake,
He prayed, "O Lord, just lead me home.
Safely, for goodness sakes."

As soon as he drove into the driveway,
He knew he was as good as dead.
He knew it was all over for him,
No matter what he done or said.

His parents were so happy that he was safe.
There were policemen everywhere,
Caring friends, and nosy neighbors,
Even the news media was there.

The next morning he was headline news,
His face was all over the TV.
Runaway car drove home by kid.
He was a celebrity.

His friends at school gathered around
To hear about the slipping of the brake,
Not realizing it could have been fatal
And that it was a horrible mistake.

All the heroism publicity
Left a very damaging scar.
Friends of his, younger and older,
Just had to drive a car.

Too young to get a license,
No money to buy some wheels.
The only other option open
Is to go out and steal.

What Will You Do Then?

Think about this, young mugger.
What will you do at last?
When Father Time catches up with you
And you can't run as fast?

What are you planning to do
When your hand is not swifter than the eye?
Sit alone by your window,
Watching the next generation go by.

Will you remember the terror you spread?
The desperate look on all those faces,
After stealing their weekly earnings,
Leaving the void and empty spaces.

Do you ever stop and realize,
That you, too, are getting older?
And the youth, coming up behind you,
Are more violent and even bolder?

What will you do when you grow old?
Be afraid to walk out of your door,
Remembering, hearing, somewhere, sometime,
That you will reap just what you sow.

Today you are the mugger,
With time and speed on your side.
But what will you do when you're older?
Just run away and hide?

Will you keep looking over your shoulder,
when you're going out and coming in?
Because then you will be the muggee.
What in the world will you do then?

Our Finest

Do you remember when the policemen
Walked the beat day and night?
Every once in a great long while,
He had to stop a fight.

During the night while strolling,
He would check locks at the stores,
Or stand up under an apartment window
To hear what went on on the different floors.

Sometimes he would carry a stick or club,
Mostly to prop up on
When his feet were tired and aching,
Or just to rest his bunions and corns.

He would stop and steer a motorist,
Back to the highway and home,
Or take a lost kid to the station,
And stuff him with ice-cream cones.

Every Friday and Saturday evening,
He would take a drunk to the tank.
To give him time to sleep it off,
And to clear his head and think.

Now the towns are overpopulated;
They've taken the cops off the beat.
Now when you need a policeman most,
They're speeding down the street.

Now they are wearing bullet-proof vests;
They carry a stick and wear a gun.
But they too are human, like you and me,
When frightened, will shoot or run.

When anyone chooses a career,
To do their best is their vow.
They train, they practice to be the best,
Or they give it their college try.

So many of our policemen
Do their best in every way,
Laying their lives on the line
Each and every day.

Then there are some policemen
For whom there is no hope,
Taking bribes, covering up,
Lying, stealing, and selling dope.

There are good cops, and bad cops.
Which one is the greater?
The ones who ask, "Can I help?"
Or the shooters, who ask questions later.

The good cops should be rewarded,
But how can you tell which one?
The big-hearted cop that walks the beat
Or the one that carries the gun?

Good cops, bad cops,
That is a mystery still.
That uncertain feeling you have,
When you hear that a cop has been killed.

But then there is the bully cop,
And this is truly sad.
He does his dirty underhanded deeds
And makes the other cops look bad.

What the Hell Do You Expect?

You took us from our native land;
You stowed us on your ship's deck.
You didn't care if we lived or died;
You would get more, so what the heck.

You put us on the auction block;
You sold us by the peck.
You worked us until we died;
What the hell did you expect?

The morsels of food you gave us
Were not enough to sustain a child.
But you expected a man-sized day from us.
Just work, keep singing, and smile.

You worked us from before the sunrise,
To the setting of the same.
You took away our heritage and courage;
You even changed our name.

We worked through the icy winters,
Then under the burning summer sun.
We fought the fight, we ran the race,
But the battle is still to be won.

You would not allow us to learn to read,
Nor write, or figure, but what the heck.
Only if it was for your convenience,
So what the hell do you expect?

You raped our mothers and sisters,
Castrated our fathers, hung them by the neck.
All it meant was a slave is gone;
We'll buy more, so what the heck.

We were treated worse than the animals,
It was a shame, a total disgrace.
There was no such thing as a funeral,
Because we would be replaced.

You took away our heritage and dignity,
You sold our families, destroyed our pride.
The only pay we got from you,
Were the stripes upon our hide.

Then along came the great white father,
With human kindness and great respect,
Set us free to find our way.
With the noose of ignorance still around our necks.

Blacks and Hispanics

It is said that Blacks and Hispanics
Are the lowest people on earth,
That the world has not been the same
Since the day of their birth.

But did you ever stop to talk to one,
To learn of their fears and doubts?
How they bleed when they are hurt,
For things they have to do without?

Do you realize that they too, get lonely,
When they are all alone?
To whom or where can they turn,
When all their hopes are gone?

Do you ever wonder how they feel,
When they're doing their very best?
Knowing that they're being watched,
And forever being put to a test.

Tested for so many things
That they were never taught.
Like how to fly a super jet,
While flying is just a thought.

They want to eat in nice restaurants,
But they can't spare the dime.
But you think that's impossible,
With them robbing and looting all the time.

They feel the same as you and me;
They too want a piece of the pie,
While they are down here on earth,
Not just up there in the sky.

So where do they go when they are lonely,
Cold, frightened, and want to be warm?
They go to the only haven they know.
Home, and into their loving spouse's arms.

For that too, they are criticized,
And have been for a while.
Instead of looking for another job,
They go home and make another child.

A baby, they know, they can't afford,
So what do you think they will do?
Go out and get in the welfare line,
Like all the Blacks and Hispanics do.

Sharecropping

Sharecropping is a form of slavery,
Nothing but agony and pain.
You till the soil, and raise the crops,
And the owner sits back and gains.

Since you are supposed to be a free man,
You send your children to school to learn
That there has to be a better way;
Learn to live off what you earn.

That there is a better way,
To work as a free man and thrive.
Take the good and bad on the chin,
And struggle to survive.

Sending your children out to school,
Because you want them to learn,
But when they find out what this sharing is,
The owner becomes concerned.

"I heard your boy is doing good in school,
and education can be a great tool.
But now it's time he learned about the farm,
And you say, he wants to go off to school.

"Everybody wants to go to school,
But that makes a boy turn soft.
And you're becoming an old man now;
He's got to take over where you leave off.

"I know your boy wants to go to school,
But there are a lot of things worse.
I've shared everything I own with you,
And somebody's going to pay me first.

"You live rent-free in my old shack.
I buy the seed and furnish the plow.
Last year when your food ran out,
I let you have my prized sow.

"You've got to remember I am the owner,
And God knows I try to be fair.
You couldn't get a better break,
From anyone, anywhere.

"I gave your wife the store-bought scraps,
To trim her children's clothes.
I bet you can't begin to figure
How much I paid for those.

"Do you remember how good your wife looks,
And how dignified she acts
When she uses them store-bought scraps
To trim those fertilizer sacks?

"Don't you forget that blue serge suit
That I just passed on to you.
I only wore that suit ten years;
It's almost as good as new.

"Remember when your wife had that baby,
And she got down mighty low.
You know that's going to cost you;
My wife had to scrub her own floor.

"And don't forget you owe me,
That time I sent you into town,
To pick up the fertilizer,
When you broke the wagon down.

"I know you can't forget
When I gave you that advance,
Money to buy new work shoes,
A hat, a shirt, and pants.

"So if your son is thinking about leaving,
Don't make another plan;
Nobody is going anywhere,
Until my money is in my hand.

"So your son wants to go away to school?
That's impossible, you see.
You and him working day and night,
Can't pay back all that you owe me.

"You are an old man now;
Your wife, too, is getting on.
Who is going to run the farm,
If your son is off and gone?

"But I want to be a fair man,
And maybe there is a way.
I think we might break even,
If you work a hundred years and a day."

Unbiased

I get along with all races of people;
We live together like sugar and water.
But the friendship ends, I tell you, friend,
When it's your black son, and my white daughter.

I walk hand in hand with every man,
Just like law and order,
But I draw the line every time,
When it's your black son, and my white daughter.

I don't mind them attending the same school,
Nor within reason having fun,
As long as there is a distance kept,
Between my white daughter, and your black son.

If my white son should meet your black daughter,
And they should get along,
I can't see anything wrong with that;
Anyway, what harm can be done?

But now you see your son is black,
Ill mannered, and acts a little crazy.
He's spineless as a jelly fish,
But most of all he's lazy.

On the other hand my daughter is white;
White is right, and a whole lot smarter.
Your son is slow, but I'm sure you know,
And just won't do what he ought to.

Sure my daughter could do worse,
But to be honest, I don't know how.
She couldn't find anything lower than black,
No matter how hard she tries.

There is no reason we can't be friends,
Like God-fearing men ought to,
As long as you keep your black son,
Away from my white daughter.

But young people do the craziest things
As young ones often do,
But I would kill myself and my daughter
If she had something black like you.

The Home of the Brave

I was born in America,
The land of the free, home of the brave.
My legacy and heritage
Is somewhere in an unmarked grave.

My parents could neither read nor write,
Couldn't even identify their names.
In this land of the free and the brave,
Who do you think is to blame?

The arms of the Statue of Liberty,
In this land of the free and brave,
Reach out to everyone, except
The descendant of a slave.

My father's father's father
Worked harder than required of any man.
They had to pay twice the price
To survive on this free land.

My mother cleaned the missus's house,
Cooked, mended, and scrubbed the floor,
But in order to do their dirty work,
She had to enter through the back door.

You work all day every day
And sometimes into the night
To provide whatever you can for your own,
So that they may come up right.

You send them to school every day,
Tell them to do their best.
Although their school is secondary,
They still must pass the test.

When they leave that institution,
With a diploma in their hand,
They not only have to be good,
But better than their fellow man.

They have to work many long hours,
Operating a computer or digging a ditch.
If they are not the best on the job,
It doesn't matter which is which.

If you want to be recognized,
In the land of the free and the brave,
Don't come as a poor black,
Or be a descendant of a slave.

My Ancestors

My ancestors were born free human beings
In the land God gave us all.
With trees, fruits, and animals,
No fences, no tyrants, no walls.

Their sons were born happy men,
With a great wide range to roam.
He beat his drum, he danced and sang,
In the land he called his home.

Their sons were born Africans,
In a far, far away land.
Ill-treated, misused, and abused,
By a slave master's hand.

His sons were born slaves,
In this land across the sea.
They were sold from master to master,
In a land that was supposed to be free.

Their sons were born breeders,
To sow their seeds and multiply,
To produce many children,
For other slave masters to buy.

Their sons were born unhappy;
They, too, were used to breed,
With the strongest, healthiest females,
No matter what race or creed.

I grieve when I think that my ancestors,
Old, overworked, and forlorn,
Saw their children being sold or killed
Until they were all gone.

Their sons were born without a country,
Neither here nor from whence they came.
They were known by whom their masters were.
That's how they got their names.

Their sons were born niggers,
Not knowing a rightful name.
Stripped of his heritage and dignity,
Not knowing from whence he came.

Their sons were born as colored men.
They could neither read nor write.
They worked all day in the burning sun
And prayed for freedom by night.

Their sons were born Negroes,
But now they are supposed to be free.
His blood is so mixed and mangled up,
They're not sure what they are supposed to be.

Their sons were born black men
In the land of the free and the brave,
But it seems the higher he rises,
The more he stays a slave.

Their sons were born Afro-Americans,
Trying to educate themselves, you see.
Educate yourself and you'll be as good
As any man can be.

As I think back on my ancestry,
Sometimes I find myself in tears.
Still the battle goes on and on,
And will go on for years.

Be proud, African-Americans.
Tell the world and yourself you're good.
No other race of people on earth
Can understand, or stand, what you stood.

Pigs' Feet

Let me tell you about pigs' feet;
This is how the story goes.
The poor black enslaved people
Were only given the guts, feet, and nose.

Just imagine serving the master's table
With hog nose, which was called the snout.
He would whip the maid and hang the cook,
And throw the whole mess out.

Think of serving him a trotter,
Just to see how fast you can run.
Because when he grabs that whip to you,
You'll try to catch up with the sinking sun.

Now try serving him hog guts—
Today we call them chitterlings.
If you don't know what horse-whipping is,
Try serving them if you're willing.

If you start feeling daring,
And to see what mood the master's in,
Try serving him some spare ribs,
Without removing the skin.

Whenever hog-killing time came around,
The slaves would rejoice,
For soon there would be good eating,
Even if the cuts weren't choice.

As far as the master was concerned,
There was bacon, ribs, shoulder, and ham.
Just give him that, without the fat;
About the rest he didn't give a damn.

They learned how to salt and smoke the pork,
To be thankful to God and pray,
For the pigs' head, skin, and feet,
Meant survival for another day.

In Line

I went to the store to pick up some bread,
And the checkout line was so long.
I wondered if I really wanted it,
And what in the world could be wrong.

I went over to the phone company,
To pay what was due on the phone.
I found myself nodding in the line,
So I got out of the line and went on home.

How in the world can I get ahead?
Today everything is a grind.
It's impossible to get ahead,
Standing in the back of a line.

I went to the doctor's office;
The line was outside the door.
Every seat there was taken,
So I just sat there on the floor.

I was so tired and disgusted,
I had to take my time and think.
And nothing makes the head clearer
Than a good stiff drink.

So I strolled around to the liquor store,
Not thinking about what I would find.
You hit the nail right on the head;
I found a longer line.

I went to the unemployment office,
And patiently waited in line;
The interviewer said, as I approached the desk,
"Sorry, you'll have to come back another time."

When I think of the situation,
I feel just like crying.
How in the world can I get ahead,
Standing in the back of the line?

I stopped in to see my banker,
Trying to get a loan.
I looked at the line and shook my head;
Come my turn, the money will be gone.

As my situation became more desperate,
Now I'm going out of my mind.
I had to resort to the last resort;
I had to stand in the welfare line.

So this is the situation;
Face it come rain or shine.
If you're going to do it the American way,
You've got to stand in line.

Credit Card

Finally I am a man;
I can do as I please.
No more "Can I do this and that?"
No more groveling on my knees.

No more weekly curfew.
No more running off to school.
All of that is behind me now.
I've learned the golden rule.

I landed myself a good job.
Money stashed away that I don't use.
Plenty of time stowed up on the job,
So I decided to take a cruise.

I called a travel agency;
The first thing they wanted to know.
"How long do you want to stay?
And where do you want to go?"

I had never called a travel agency.
I had never been anywhere.
So I just told her to book me,
On anything, going anywhere.

"Sir, do you have a passport?
But first your credit card."
With all the money in my pocket.
That question struck me odd.

"Look here, Miss, money is no object.
Just book me on a trip.
I don't need a credit card,
With all this money on my hip."

"Sir, I'm sure you have money,
And that's all well and good.
People don't travel with money nowadays;
The credit card is understood."

I applied for a Master Card,
Visa, American Express, and others.
Now that I had them all,
There wasn't anything I could not cover.

I took a trip to China,
Spent time in Japan.
Gondolaed in Italy,
And visited castles in England.

I bought all kind of fancy clothes,
Ate in fancy restaurants.
If I wanted it, I got it;
There was no such thing as can't.

Oh, but then came pay-back time.
Tell me what do you think.
I had overcharged on the credit cards,
And was overdrawn at the bank.

I asked for overtime on the job,
And even sought part-time work.
An educated man like me,
What a joke, what a jerk.

So when you decide you're a man
And want to live a life of ease,
Take it from me, I've been there;
Leave credit cards alone please.

So when you think you know it all,
because you have learned the golden rule,
Make sure you have taken a course at
A "How to use a credit card" school.

What Cocaine Done to Me

Sit back and I will tell you a story,
About today's biggest lie,
About how cocaine destroys a life.
I will tell you what happens, and why.

I saw an old friend the other day.
I wanted to cry, I must say.
He looked so sad and forlorn,
A hundred years old, if a day.

I didn't want to be rude to him.
I just thanked God he had survived.
He was such a horrible sight to see.
He looked more dead than alive.

"What happened to you?" I had to know.
I guess to him I sounded dumb.
"Nothing," he said, "why do you ask?"
Looked like he had been hit by a bomb.

He saw the concerned look on my face,
And heard the care in my voice.
Then he started telling me his story,
As if he had no choice.

He began, "The last time I saw you,
I just could not wait.
I had just gotten out of school,
And everything was great.

"I landed a very good job,
Got married and had a child.
Everything was going just great,
And that lasted for a while.

"Then I ran in to an old friend of mine,
From my old neighborhood.
He said he was so glad to see me,
And he could see I was doing good.

"He suggested that I come to visit him,
Whenever I could find the time.
Don't forget to bring your family with you;
Then, too, you can meet mine.

"So one day I was just cruising by,
And just decided I would stop by.
That was the beginning of my mistake.
That's when I started living the lie.

"We sat and talked and kidded around,
And remembered the good old days.
We talked about the fun we had,
Before going our separate ways.

"He invited me to a party;
I must have been insane.
He introduced me to his friends,
And that awful drug cocaine.

"But I was a man of dignity,
Of prestige, and I had class.
So I decided to try it this one time;
It would be my first time and my last.

"At first I was stopping by once a week;
Then it was once or twice.
Every time I left the neighborhood,
Oh, man, I felt so nice.

"My wife and my co-workers
Started to nag and complain.
I didn't care what they said,
As long as I had my cocaine.

"This cocaine had gotten so good to me,
I started taking off from work.
My boss called me into his office
And he sounded just like a jerk.

" 'Young man, you are such an asset,
I would hate to have to let you go.
But your work has gotten so raggedly,
That everyone in the office knows.

" 'You take some time off from work,
And get help for yourself.
You got yourself into this mess,
And you can't blame anyone else.'

"Still I got up every morning,
Took off as I had always done.
Go out and find my buddies.
Get some cocaine and have some fun.

"When my money started running out,
My buddies ran out too.
No job, no friends, no cocaine.
What am I going to do?

"Now that I look back on my life.
I feel dirty, I feel cheap.
When I think of what has happened to me,
I can only think back and weep.

"I was a good employee and husband.
Check my record and you will see.
I really didn't do anything,
But look at what cocaine has done to me."

A Done Deal

Anyone can give up and die,
But death is a done deal.
So fight with all your might to hold on.
It takes vigor, it takes zest and zeal.

Everyone knows illness takes its toll,
But you have to put up a fight.
When illness punches you high and low,
You come back with a left and right.

When old age starts creeping in,
Eat proper and exercise.
Everyone does not win the race,
Only the one who tries.

Then too there is depression,
And depression attacks us all.
But when depression shoots its best shot,
Stand firm; show it you refuse to fall.

When someone loses a loved one,
It hurts so deeply, the pain is so real.
You know for sure you can't go on,
Because this is surely a done deal.

But then you must remember,
That Christ died for our sin.
He fought a good fight and even died,
But death is not the end.

Losing your worldly possessions
Is enough to make you give in.
But just like Job, you had it once,
You will get it again.

So push illness and depression aside,
And welcome old age in.
The older you get, the longer you live,
And as long as you live, you win.

Going Home

I went to a home-going the other day
To pay the last respects to a friend
Who had run a great race,
Who had fought a good fight,
But now the battle is at an end.

Oh, there were floods of tears,
Tears of joy, and tears of laughter.
My friend had finally crossed the line,
Into the life hereafter.

As we lament over this body,
My friend has gone on to the reward.
As the undertaker lowers the body down,
The spirit is up there with the Lord.

Be sad when they come into the world.
That's when the pain and suffering start,
Over rough mountains, down through pitfalls,
Until the day, you, this life depart.

How can we be sad for them?
Finally they are free from pain.
They have been out in the storm so long,
At last they're in from the rain.

No longer can we walk and talk together,
And the pain and loss will be hard,
But I will keep on doing as I did then.
I'll keep walking and talking with God.

Everything our Savior does,
There is His time and reason.
Enjoy it, make the most of it,
Because it's only for a season.

Don't look for my friend in the field,
As if my friend is just going out to plow.
My friend has tilled, planted, and harvested.
My friend has gone home now.

The Christ in Christmas

You start your Christmas club savings
The first month of the year
In order to buy Christmas presents
For everyone you hold dear.

You make yourself a mental note
Of all the new friends you find
To add to your next Christmas list
But does Christ ever cross your mind?

You work real hard to pay the bills
That you made Christmas past.
The time is spent; the day is gone.
Only bills and memories last.

Early in the year we remember,
Or so the story goes,
How Christ died on the cross
And Easter Sunday he arose.

Too we remember Thanksgiving day,
When friends and strangers meet
To thank Christ for his blessings
And bountiful food to eat.

Thinking of last year's dinner,
But this will be the best one yet.
Old recipes from years gone by,
The dinner no one will be able to forget.

Sadly there was a family
That remembered our Savior by name.
They overwired their Christmas tree,
And their house went up in flame.

Daily we should remember Jesus Christ.
No special occasion or reason.
Jesus Christ is our Savior and Lord.
He is the reason for the season.

Jesus Christ is the sweetest name,
The greatest gift you will ever find.
Put Christ at the top of your list,
And forever present in your mind.

The Christ in Christmas means Savior.
Take it with you the whole year through.
Then you will possess the world's greatest gift.
Merry Christmas to you.